D1602462

THE HONEST ACCOUNT

OF A MEMORABLE LIFE

AN APOCRYPHAL

GOSPEL

THE HONEST
ACCOUNT OF A
MEMORABLE LIFE
AN APOCRYPHAL
GOSPEL
BY
REYNOLDS PRICE

NORTH CAROLINA WESLEYAN

COLLEGE PRESS

Published by:
North Carolina Wesleyan College Press
3400 North Wesleyan Boulevard
Rocky Mount, North Carolina
27804

FOREWORD

At Duke University in the spring term of 1993, I led a new seminar in the gospels of Mark and John. All sixteen students were undergraduates—a few with considerable prior awareness of New Testament literature, most with virtually none. Through the first two months, line by line in my own plain translations, we discussed the historical, narrative and religious connotations of Mark (the oldest life of Jesus) and John (the most mysterious). I call the two gospels *lives* since, whatever their theological aims, Mark and John are first of all brief attempts to record the crucial events and the meaning of a single temporal earthly existence; and modern attempts to deny that aim are blind to the universal motive and history of narrative.

We next read, briskly, the gospels of Matthew and Luke. Then in the Polebridge Press edition of *The Complete Gospels*, we read the more cogent apocryphal documents pertaining to Jesus. At mid-term as we prepared to write final seminar papers—we'd each write a new apocryphal gospel—the students and I agreed upon a common set of sources for our ground plans. We'd be free to use the four canonical gospels, the Acts of the Apostles (the other surviving first-century New Testament narrative), the undisputed letters of Paul and those other New Testament letters which may at least have originated in the first generation of men and women who knew Jesus of Nazareth.

A reader may wonder why I set such a task when we already have four impressive gospels, two of which stand a good chance of proceeding directly or at only second-hand from eye-witnesses. The simplest answer—and one that has lain behind the thousands of attempts on Jesus that have crowded libraries for the past two millennia—is that the life and its effect on history are so magnetic in their mystery as to demand ceaseless watch and question. A more precise explanation of why I set my seminar to work on further attempts would center on a feeling that I share with most students of Matthew, Mark, Luke and John—they each offer credible acts and speeches that are found in no other early source and that beg to be set side-by-side in a single account. The famous *Diatesseron* of Tatian, completed in the second century, is only the first of such attempts at a satisfying harmony of all known gospel themes.

With some such aim then, and on that common base of evidence, each of us began to write an apocryphal gospel—I'd made myself a working member from the start. By the end of term, the students had produced the most interesting set of papers I'd received in thirty-five years of teaching; and as I expected, their gospels were a good deal freer than mine in arranging, discarding or elaborating the oldest evidence and hints.

My gospel, on the contrary, hews closely to Mark's generally convincing chronology for the life, work and death of Jesus— an outline that seems to come from Mark's main informant, who was almost surely Peter. Into that loose-limbed itinerary, I've inserted certain events and speeches from Matthew, Luke and John as well as the apparently genuine but unattached episode of Jesus' response to the woman taken in adultery (it is not a part of the gospel of John, though it's often placed there). I've made such inclusions occur only when they seem indispensable for the fullest understanding of Jesus that we can reach if we try to keep faith with the oldest witnesses. I set the additions at points where they serve both a narrative and an emotional logic and do part-justice to at least two aspects of Jesus' nature—his deep compassion and ferocious anger.

Such a shuffling of sources is frowned upon by many New Testament scholars as disruptive of what they take to be the mutually exclusive errands of the four evangelists. I dissent from their prohibition, as did most early Christian writers, for one large reason. The first three gospels may well have been built by just such a process of conflation and interleaving; and since the most inexplicable acts of Jesus are described with a flat-footed refusal to heighten their marvels, most of those events mix well with one another. From whichever gospel we draw them, they seem so starkly matter-of-fact that in general they lie together easily.

Where I rearrange or, rarely, invent a piece of bridgework—moving Jesus from place to place in Palestine, say, or linking separate acts in what seem possible ways—I do so in the manner of my originals, with a minimum of embroidery. Faced with imposing memories that may often have reached the writers with no geographical or chronological context, they built the best homes they could manage for such detached timbers.

When I imagine the conception and birth of Jesus, for instance, and when I set three invented speeches into the mouths of his family and pupils (Joseph at the birth, Peter at the transfiguration, Mary Magdalene at the tomb), I do so with guidance from those few apocryphal stories which seem profound in their guesswork—my main hint comes from the impressive first-person nativity speech of Joseph in the Proto-gospel of James. I rely on the reader's native wit to note that in places my history is metaphoric. I likewise add the odd detail from early sources. From Paul's claim in First Corinthians 15 that the risen Jesus appeared to James his brother and to "the Twelve," I've deduced an appearance to Judas his traitor. From other early accounts that may well preserve fact, I've suggested that Jesus had worked at the blacksmith's forge and that Zebedee's son John sold fish to the High Priest in Jerusalem; and when a modern archeological finding has seemed relevant, or an observation from my own two visits to Israel, I've included it. Throughout I emulate the original Greek in avoiding punctuation except where confusion might result. It's a virtue of such clean prose to keep a reader watchful and to drive off the inattentive.

My hope is that a discerning reader will note my few inventions as careful meditations on a quantity of bedrock history that exceeds the facts we possess for any other ancient life whose force survives in our civilization. We after all know as much or more of the life of Jesus of Nazareth as we know of such clamorous lives as Ramses II's, Alexander the Great's or even Augustus Caesar's; and we maim our good luck in having so much and our common sense in gauging its worth when we fail to grant the wealth of our sources.

As Mark, John, Matthew and Luke each transform speech and act into story with the purpose of discovering both a life and that life's meaning, so my own dutiful mosaic finds a figure deep in its surface. That figure is of course shaped and colored by my own predilections; but a brief summary here will, I hope, show my bias as sane and justified.

My version of the life and meaning has a spine like this. In the reign of the Roman emperor Augustus, a young man—intended by God as his Son—grows up obscurely in northern Palestine. From early years he ponders the aim of his life and confirms his sense of unique Sonship in the revelatory moment of his baptism by John, a desert prophet. Jesus ratifies that Sonship, to his own amazement and doubt, in a crowded tour of teaching and healing through the towns and farms of his home district, Galilee. His doubts are resolved when he learns, in a moment of strange exaltation on the heights of Mount Hermon, that his fated mission is the largest in history—the blood redemption of humankind from its willful fall into self and greed. Confirmed in his surety of purpose, he then descends with his baffled pupils to Jerusalem, challenges both the Temple authorities and the Roman overlords; and (after an hour of terrible fear), he dies at their joined hands, is buried on a Friday evening and rises bodily from the dead two mornings later. In uncanny but convincing appearances, he rallies his frightened and scattered pupils for a campaign of mercy, warning and hope to all human creatures—a campaign that continues today.

The evidence seems to me to permit that one legible pattern among innumerable others—the sight of a single human life lived nearer to the Maker's mind than any other life yet heard of, west of the Jordan river at least and through all western history till now.

THE HONEST ACCOUNT

OF A MEMORABLE LIFE

AN APOCRYPHAL

GOSPEL

IT BEGAN WITH a girl who was loved by God. The girl was named Mary and was aged fourteen. She'd been promised in childhood to the builder Joseph but her mother Anna was wasting with sickness and Mary had Joseph's leave to stay home till her mother was walking again or dead. So the girl lived on in her mother's house which was one dry room that backed on a cave. Her father had been a priest of the Temple but died years back in the battering sun as he walked from Jerusalem down to Bethlehem, a town of six hundred souls, the home of King David dead a long thousand years.

On a spring afternoon in the year before King Herod died in filth and worms Mary brought water in from the well and was kneeling beside her sleeping mother to wipe the feverish face and arms when a silent voice gripped the girl's strong hand. She'd heard the voice twice before but only in music, a high keen distant chanting.

Now the chant was distant words so high that the girl looked down to see if fear had waked her mother.

Anna lay still on her clean pallet.

The first words again and again were a name, *Sweet Mary*.

The girl went on soothing her mother. Mary had known her own beauty for two years but this was a prideful demon to shun.

The next high words were separate but clear. *You - God's choice - your son - his son.*

Baffled but calm as she'd never been Mary faced the door to

3

the world and said *Yes* with a single nod. When her hand came back to her mother's brow her mother was dead.

Mary spent an hour washing the body and wrapping it in the linen they'd saved for this last purpose. Then she stood and walked toward Joseph's shop.

Joseph lived in the back and slept on boards. But at dark that day he moved in beside young Mary at last—the law allowed it after betrothal—and they were married by midsummer though only in law. Near her there in her old home Joseph slowly learned of the terror planted in her womb and growing daily. Through the long wait his pallet lay apart from Mary's by the reach of his arm and there were days that summer and fall when Joseph pressed iron nails deep into his hands to let out part of the pain he felt but never told. This girl had been taken and used to the dregs before he touched her.

So EARLY THAT winter, a freezing night when Mary called Joseph's name in the dark before the pain broke from her in groans Joseph brought the lamp, saw she was wet but clean of blood, then ran uphill to the midwife's house.

As the midwife stepped out onto the path she gave him her own jar to fill at David's spring.

Long after they moved to Nazareth in Galilee where Joseph's brother Clopas owned land and a building business, when Joseph would stop to watch Mary's boy—with Mary's likeness in the lean dark face—he'd recall the strangeness that came down on him as he trotted home that night with water. *My heart had seized up in my chest. A nighthawk hung in the air beyond me all but in reach. Through the open door of a house in lamplight I saw three men and a dwarfish girl stalled in the cold, bread in their fingers aimed at their lips but still as bones.*

4

Yet when I looked the stars were wheeling. Then suddenly blood roared again in my ears and I went toward home.

At home the midwife had led Mary back to the cave that served as a stable and pen. The colt and the hens had warmed the space and when Joseph bent to look in the door the boy was already born and dugging his mother's breast.

Her eyes had found their lifelong sight but she looked to Joseph and told him the boy would be named Jesus.

JOSEPH RAISED the boy, the first in a line of five sons and three daughters. He led the sons to the synagogue school where they surpassed him by learning their letters and reading the law and prophets on sight. He found good husbands for the girls.

And the eldest boy, the one from Bethlehem, repaid the training Joseph gave him. After he and his brothers left school for work in the family trade Jesus would go to the rabbi at night and read the law and prophets till late. Before he was grown he knew them well and many nights while his kinsmen slept Jesus walked alone in the hills. He could look down on the plain of Jezreel where God and his armies had fought Israel's enemies and where the great battle of the last days would rage. He could look to the lights of Herod Antipas's capital Sepphoris three miles from Nazareth—a marble city with a palace, a theater, baths and a temple to the deified man Augustus Caesar. The boy learned the story of all he saw.

Every spring he went up with his family to eat the Passover feast in Jerusalem honoring the night when God's mercy spared the slave hovels where Hebrews lived in Pharaoh's Egypt but killed the first-born in their masters' homes. Old King Herod's new Temple in Jerusalem, built on the site of Solomon's Temple, was all but finished after decades of work. And there among its ivory and gold young Jesus talked with any priest or lawyer who would hear his questions and feed his thirst to learn if God was truly the Father of all.

Back in Nazareth he showed keen skill at the smithing forge among his brothers who were masons and carvers. And from the day when Joseph died young Jesus bore the first son's duty to tend his mother who at forty was hunched with all she'd borne as God's choice—the lean girl Mary who was bent now and worn.

BUT WHEN JESUS passed his thirtieth year he turned his back on the home he'd known. His mother and all his brothers and sisters stayed in Nazareth but in the spring Jesus walked south through Galilee and on down the banks of the Jordan through country held by Rome now and ruled at the will of Tiberius Caesar by the puppet sons of old Herod the Great. Their moves were watched by the merciless eye of Pontius Pilate, Caesar's legate in Palestine. When Jesus reached a bend in the river near Jericho he saw the man he'd come to find, a man whose fame had reached even Nazareth.

It was near sundown and the mob who daily came from Jerusalem—lawyers, priests, rich women, whores, wretches—had ridden southwest back up through hills toward the golden Temple or were cooking over their fires on the east bank. The famous man that Jesus had come for was John the Baptizer. John had cried out here since the winter solstice against all evil hearts around him. He warned of God's taut patience and wrath, the coming down of God's last plan in fire and terror. John would say "One stronger than I is coming whose sandal I'm not fit to loosen. The winnowing fan is in his hand. He'll utterly sweep his threshing floor and gather the good wheat into his barn. He'll burn the chaff in roaring fire. Take shelter now. Thresh your own grain."

John offered a ritual washing from sin, for readiness. Near dusk as it was John was still at the edge of the river this day, still waiting in his camel skins. To the eye he made a credible image of the prophet Elijah whose return was expected as the near forerunner of God's anointed. That longed-for man, God's son the Messiah, would roll Rome into the Roman sea, mount Israel's throne and open souls to God's whirlwind—God's hand in history redeeming time. What John was waiting to welcome had come. Jesus beyond him was surely the man. John sensed him on sight, beckoned the younger man toward him, then forded the river to the waist-deep midst.

Jesus stripped and waded to meet John.

John met his eyes with half the blaze of recognition but when Jesus gave no nod or sign, then John's eyes faltered. So he seized Jesus by the hair and buried him backward in the stream.

When he drew Jesus up John's eyes still questioned him.

But Jesus faced the dusky zenith. Whatever John or the cooking stragglers saw or heard Jesus watched the sky torn open above, a white dove sifting down through the air and what he heard was that same voice his mother heard but kept in secret. It said *You are my only Son.*

FOR MORE than a month Jesus walked alone in the desert past Jericho, the crags and wastes of the hot Dead Sea, Earth's deepest pit. He thought his way the best he could through what he'd seen and heard that dusk with John above him in the cold brown river, God's meaning for him and the time he'd have. The time felt short.

Vipers, jackals, a starved lion and swarms of flies crossed Jesus' path in the sun-struck days. A flock of ravens circled his head too famished to caw but even when his own hunger sapped him and he was sleeping nights in gullies with no more cover than his seamless coat no creature more than sniffed his hand or licked the dry soles of his feet.

What came nearer to harming Jesus in those days was the tempting spirit that came his way in numerous forms. One form wore his mother's face and led a child by the hand toward him saying "This is my son"—the child was himself. Another form likewise wore Jesus' face but was old and smiling with sons and daughters that bore his traits and tended his age. A third was all the human beauty he'd known till now, all the hair he'd touched.

Eventually on the fortieth day Jesus fended the spirit off. By then he was high on a peak above Jericho. When the final tempter melted in air Jesus howled to the rocks, gnawed thorny weeds and turned his lean face back to the north but not toward home. His aim was the harp-shaped lake of Kinnereth set in the hills of south Galilee though he hardly knew what his mind or hands, his power or weakness, would do once there.

As HE WALKED on the lake's north shore and hills he told whoever would pause to listen to the news he'd learned alone in the desert—that the reign of God would break in on them any day, that they must turn from waste and hatred to ready themselves for a fierce coming judgment and then for the reign of love and mercy. His hearers were farmers and fishermen, their wives and children, the occasional rabbi and village crank, the whores and cheats.

From among them he chose two pairs of brothers. The first were Simon son of Jonah and his brother Andrew, then John the son of Zebedee and his brother James—all four were fishermen. The sons of Zebedee were heirs to their father's thriving business which sold dried fish to prosperous households as far south as Jericho and Jerusalem, a two-day trek. Even the High Priest bought their fish at his backdoor downhill from the Temple.

The way Jesus called them was the first strange thing. One late spring evening he walked along the strand near their town Capernaum on the lake's north shore and as he saw them beaching boats and mending nets he told them "Come. We'll fish for humans."

For reasons they never plumbed the four men dropped their work and followed him. Where he led them first was to Simon and Andrew's house. He was weak with hunger.

But Simon's mother-in-law was down with a lingering fever and not till Jesus went to her pallet, crouched beside her whispering, then took her hand and raised her up did she have the strength to cook a supper for the five men newly bound together as teacher and pupils.

In that small town word leaked at once that the teacher Jesus had brought Simon's mother from the edge of death and by the time the men finished eating a crowd had gathered at the narrow door.

Among them was a leper too grim to watch. The crowd stood back when the leper pressed through Simon's door to stand above where Jesus sat. He said to Jesus "You can heal me if you want to."

Jesus stayed in place but met the man's eyes, managed a smile and said "I want to."

The leper was healed. By the time he'd run out into the street his open sores were sealing and fading.

Then the crowd rushed to enter the house—there was only room for a dozen people.

But Jesus made his way out through them. The synagogue was twenty yards north. He led the way there and was trying to pray when a man in the milling crowd behind him was flung to the floor by a demon seizure.

The man writhed, foamed, then stretched out rigid with his eyes rolled back and his hands clenched so hard the blood leaked from them.

Jesus tried to go on praying but he finally turned and seeing the man he called out loudly to the demon that held him "Come out now!"

The demon cringed hard and howled. "Have mercy, Jesus. We know who you are—"

Jesus stopped it from telling the truth by saying "Silence! Come out now!"

With a last shudder the demon obeyed and soon the man was upright and thankful.

So Jesus had no choice but to go back out to the street and heal whoever brought him their bodies. He failed no one and was white with exhaustion when the last man, woman and child were gone and he could rest on Simon's floor. Till now the demons had not obeyed him and the new power shook him in dreams all night.

WORD OF that night swept the whole lake shore and the hills behind. And while Jesus meant to go on telling people of the imminent breaking in of God and the need for love and mercy meanwhile he was met in every town and field by mobs of the sick who silenced his teaching. Even healthy people brought him their cripples in carts and barrows.

Balked as he was he felt real anguish and pity at the sight of the power of demons on Earth and he healed when he could, when he knew he was trusted. Even back home in Capernaum he could hardly rest.

One day he was inside teaching his pupils and a few of the lawyers who'd come from Jerusalem to check on rumors. The door was shut on the crowd outside but a pair of desperate men from the hills climbed onto the house with their paralyzed brother and broke through the mud and straw roof with sticks. Then they lowered their brother's pallet near the spot where Jesus sat and they begged him for healing.

At once the lawyers reminded Jesus that this was the Sabbath and work was forbidden.

So Jesus faced the cripple and said "Son, your sins are forgiven."

The cripple had hardly come for that but he nodded thanks.

The lawyers were amused, then appalled. "No one forgives real sin but God."

The cripple likewise nodded at that.

But Jesus faced him smiling and said "So you know the Son of Man has power to forgive all sins—" He raised his hand and the cripple was amazed. Jesus said "Stand, take your cot and go."

The man walked out on two sound legs toward his brothers bawling for joy outside.

But the lawyers were scandalized and left. By their lights this man was not only breaking the laws of God but was dangerously attracting mobs that might yet boil into one more round of the frequent bloody quarrels with Rome. From that day they and Herod's henchmen all plotted to silence Jesus or end him. This was Herod Antipas, Rome's puppet in Galilee, Samaria and Perea, a man whom Jesus called "the Fox." He'd stopped John the Baptizer for now—John was jailed for denouncing Herod's marriage to his living brother's wife.

So Jesus stayed on the restless move choosing pupils to add to the four from Capernaum. In the final group of Twelve were Simon who was later called Peter, Andrew his brother, John and James the sons of Zebedee whom Jesus called the Sons of Thunder, Philip, Bartholomew, Matthew, Thomas, James son of Alpheus, Thaddeus, Simon the Zealot and Judas Iscariot. There were also women who followed his wanderings providing for him out of their belongings. Among them was Mary from the town of Magdala on the lake. Jesus had flushed seven demons from her body and her thanks were endless.

As they walked through the towns of Galilee Jesus healed where he could and tried to make people hear the heat of his call to change. God's reign was near, maybe on them already. How could they know of the fullness of time, of God's impatience to love them again—they with their lives still strapped in harness and their eyes on the ground? They must love God above all and then their neighbors in complete fairness with minds pure of pride or greed.

Once when he sat in a boat offshore to speak to a crowd without being mobbed Jesus felt God's nearness beating so hard that he cried "Look, I've come to set fire to the world. See how my hands are bound till it blazes!"

But some of the sickest plunged in the water and started toward him.

The pupils oared the boat farther out, set sail and went toward the eastern shore where towns were sparse and wilderness stretched. Toward evening a storm broke. The boat was swamping but Jesus was sleeping curled in the stern. The pupils shook him— "Can't you see we're drowning? Do something now."

Jesus looked at the waves, smiled and said "Be still."

The water was calm long before the pupils could trust their safety.

But as they landed near sunset Jesus saw first thing a man on the brow of the rise ahead.

The man was naked and dirty with wild hair. His hands and legs were locked in shackles but he'd broken the chains.

A boy on the strand said the man had been crazy all the boy's life, that he lived in the graves, cut at himself with flints and shells and ate raw fish which he caught by hand.

The pupils wanted to put back out—a graveyard dweller was impure to touch.

But Jesus jumped from the boat and walked in a straight line toward the man.

The man held still but when Jesus neared the man cried "Back! Stay back, oh God!"

Jesus came to him and held out a hand. When the man recoiled Jesus asked him his name.

An entire tribe of demons was in him refusing to answer. But when Jesus raised his voice to press them they finally said "Our name is Legion." They spoke like a chorus of bats in the dark that was rushing in.

But Jesus kept saying "Out, come out" in a steady voice.

When the demons knew they had to obey they spoke again and begged to be sent into some young pigs that were rooting nearby.

Jesus nodded.

The demons flew straight into the pigs.

The pigs shied, then stampeded over a ledge to drown in the darkening water below.

13

But the man that had been the Legion stood peaceful. For the first time in his memory he was clean.

Jesus took off his head cloth, gave it to him and the man wrapped himself.

Then the man fell forward to worship Jesus pleading to serve him any way.

But Jesus raised him, said he should find his people now and show what God had done for him. Then Jesus walked ahead into darkness leaving the man and the baffled pupils on the strand below.

When he didn't return the pupils gave up and sailed toward home. Past midnight the wind rose and midway out they were bailing water when one of them looked and there was Jesus walking on the surface toward them. They thought he'd somehow died and was coming back as a ghost so even drowning felt preferable. They cried out for him to leave them be.

But he called across the water "I am." In their own language his words amounted to the name God gave from the burning bush when Moses asked, the name *I Am*.

That hardly calmed their terror.

But Jesus walked on into the boat and again curled up and slept in the stern. In the hours he'd spent alone in the hills he'd prayed again for guidance on the question of who he was and what God meant for his Son to do if God had truly called him Son as he rose from the Jordan in John's hands.

THE FOLLOWING DAY a synagogue leader in Capernaum tracked Jesus down, told him his little daughter was dead—the child of his heart—and begged for Jesus to hurry and call her back from sleep.

Jesus said that the leader was right "She's asleep." But the man kept begging so Jesus followed the man toward his fine house.

In the stragglers behind them was a woman who'd followed Jesus for days. She'd suffered unstanchable menstrual blood for twelve years, had been broke by doctors and was now too wretched to speak to Jesus. So she came up behind him in silence and knowing she only needed to touch him she reached and touched the hem of his coat. At once the hemorrhage stopped inside her.

Jesus had felt the power leave him. He turned and said "Who touched me then?"

The pupils said "In all this mob you expect us to know?"

By now the woman was on her knees in tears of thanks and mingled fear—would he grudge her the health?

But Jesus only touched her again and said her trust had made her well.

Then they were at the leader's door. The sound of hired mourners was strong and the women were howling.

Jesus took only Peter, James and John and pushed past the mourners to the room where the girl lay still on her mat.

She was white and cold in the dark chill room.

Again Jesus bent and took her hand. *"Talitha, koum"* he said in their language— "Girl, rise."

The girl's eyes opened. She slowly rose on unsure legs—she was twelve years old.

Her parents were speechless.

She entered their arms.

Then still to the sound of useless mourners Jesus said "Give her something to eat" and left them.

NEWS OF THAT traveled far and fast. All sorts wondered who this man was or would turn out to be.

Soon John the Baptizer sent messengers from prison and asked for a simple answer from Jesus "Are you really the one to come or not?"

Jesus waited all night, then called the messengers to him at dawn and said "Tell John this. The blind see, the lame walk, lepers are clean, the deaf hear and speak, the dead are raised and the poor learn the news of God's coming reign. Bless him who trusts me."

But when John's messengers nodded and left, Jesus turned to the pupils stunned beside him and said one more thing "Foxes have holes, the birds have nests but the Son of Man has nowhere to lay his head."

Peter and Andrew at least were offended. They'd given him room and board for weeks.

Others thought he was crazy. Some turned back home abandoning hope in what they thought he'd meant and offered— rest, power and glory in God's coming reign.

But after a troubled while the Twelve held firm around him stumped as they were.

So Jesus called them apart in secret. He gave them power over foul demons and to heal the sick. He said that they were to go through all the towns and farms of Galilee telling the hearers of God's coming reign. "Go two by two with no gold or silver, no extra shirt, just sandals and a stick and announce to Israel the good news that God is at hand. Bless the house that receives you. When a town won't receive you shake its dust from your feet. Amen I tell you it will be far better for Sodom and Gomorrah on Judgment Day than for that town.

"I'm sending you out like sheep among wolves. Be wise as snakes and guileless as doves and when they attack you here run there but never rest from telling God's news to the lost and wicked—they're welcome too. God and the angels welcome sinners more than the good. Amen I tell you you won't have

gone through the towns of Israel before the Son of Man comes
in glory."

The pupils were amazed at his expectation but they tried to
obey him and they went off in pairs.

WHILE THE TWELVE were gone Jesus heard that Herod the
Fox had killed John the Baptizer—this Fox had teeth and
would use them at will. So Jesus moved on alone through
Galilee continuing the work that was dogged by menace from
friends and haters. Yet his power worked wherever he was
trusted. In Bethsaida he met a completely blind man.

The man begged to touch him.

Jesus led the man by the hand out of town and when they
were apart he spat on the man's eyes. "Do you see anything?"

The man said "I see men that look like trees walking."

Again Jesus laid his hands on the eyes.

And the man saw clearly.

Jesus sent him home and warned him "Don't even pass back
through town."

Then while Jesus still traveled alone his mother and brothers
came from Nazareth to take him home. They'd heard the news
and thought he was crazy. When they reached where he was
he was in a house talking with serious men and women from
the district. The family sent word for him to come out.

But Jesus refused and gestured around him. "Who's my
mother and who are my brothers? Amen I tell you that my
family is all who hear and trust me. Don't think I come to
bring peace on Earth. I bring a great sword. I set a son against
his father, a daughter against her mother and a man's worst
enemies will be his own household. Remember I've come to
set fire to the world and oh I long to see it blaze!"

The brothers took his mother back to Nazareth. She was

bowed with sadness but had also seen in the eyes seated round him a reflected glare she recalled from his childhood and the distant sound of his voice had brought back the words she heard in Bethlehem when she learned of his coming, *God's choice - your son.*

THEN THE TWELVE returned from their separate travels on a day like any other day. No one could see that the reign of God had come or was closer.

Jesus saw their bafflement and said "Let's go to the wilderness and rest."

They got in the boat, sailed east again on the lake and found a secret place where Jesus could pray a little apart even from them and they could rest with no sad mobs of the sick and idle.

After a while though someone found them and a crowd gathered in the wilderness with no food or shelter.

Many wicked and outcast men were among them and Jesus told them this story about the Father's thirst for their souls. He said "A man had two sons. The younger one said to his father 'Father, give me my share of all that will come to me.' So the father divided his belongings between them. A few days later the younger son packed all he had and traveled far off. There he wasted his share in wild living and when he had spent everything a hard famine struck that place. The son was desperate so he hired himself to a man who sent him out to pasture his swine.

"The son would gladly have eaten the roots the swine ate— no one gave him anything. But once he finally came to himself he said 'My father's slaves have food to spare but I'm starving here. I'll go to my father and tell him "Father, I've sinned against Heaven and you. I'm not worthy to be called your son.

Treat me like one of your hired hands."' Then he went home-ward toward his father.

"But while he was still at a distance his father saw him and had pity. He ran and kissed him. The son said 'Father, I've sinned against Heaven and you. I'm not worthy to be called your son.' But the father said to his slaves 'Quick, bring the best coat and put it on him. Put a ring on his hand, shoes on his feet and kill the fat calf. We'll eat and be glad for this son of mine was dead and is now alive. He was lost and we've found him.' They began to be glad.

"Now the elder son was out in the field and as he got near the house he heard music and dancing. He called one of the slaves and asked what this meant and the slave told him 'Your brother is home and your father has killed the fat calf because he's got him back safe and whole.' But the elder son was angry and refused to go in.

"His father came out and begged him but he answered his father 'Look, all these years I've served you and never dis-obeyed your orders yet you never gave me even a kid so I might celebrate with my friends. But when this son of yours re-turned—the one that squandered your money on whores—you killed the fat calf for him.' So the father said to him 'Son, you're always with me and all that's mine is yours. It's fitting now to be grateful and glad for your brother was dead and is back alive. He was lost and is found.'"

When Jesus had taught them about God's hunger for their souls evening was coming and he took pity on them. He said to Philip "How are we going to feed these people?"

Philip said "We aren't. Two hundred dinars wouldn't buy bread for them."

But Andrew, Simon's brother, said "There's a boy here with five barley rolls and two fish."

So Jesus said "Make the men sit down"—there was deep green grass where they were.

The men sat down. With women and children there were some five thousand.

Jesus took the boy's rolls and fish. He thanked God for them, then passed them out to the seated crowd as much as they wanted.

When all were full the pupils picked up twelve baskets of uneaten crumbs.

And when the men took the meal as a sign that God's anointed had truly come and his reign was at hand they talked of seizing Jesus on the spot and making him king.

Jesus left quickly and the pupils followed.

FOR LACK of any safe destination he led them north into gentile country, the towns around Tyre and Sidon in Phoenicia. Even there Jesus wasn't entirely unknown and couldn't be hid. His power was evident even when muffled.

So a gentile woman found him—a Greek. She fell at his feet and begged him to heal her little daughter of a foul spirit.

Jesus said "Let the children of Israel be fed first. It's not right to take the children's bread and throw it to pups."

The woman said to him "Yes sir but pups under the table eat the children's crumbs."

Jesus smiled and told her "For that you can go home with something for your pains. The demon is gone from your daughter."

When the woman got home her daughter was well.

FROM THERE JESUS led the Twelve northeast to the flanks of Mount Hermon and the hamlets near Caesarea Philippi. More and more he was walking ahead of them or praying apart. But once on a lonely stretch of road he stopped, turned back and asked the pupils "Who do people say I am?"

They could see that he needed to know. So they told him "Some say you're Elijah, some John the Baptizer, some say you're a prophet."

Jesus pressed them. "But you—who do you say I am?"

There was silence till Simon spoke out. "You're Messiah." The Jews had long awaited Messiah, a man whose Hebrew title means *Anointed*. He was meant to free them and restore their pride in God's chosen people. Some thought he would come as a warrior chief. Some thought he'd be an eternal priest.

But as soon as Simon spoke Jesus warned the pupils to say nothing of this. Then as they walked he began to tell them that now the Son of Man must suffer many things, be refused by the lawyers and priests and be killed. "Then I will rise on the third day" he said. He spoke quite plainly.

Simon took him aside and began to warn him of such wild words—he thought Messiah was meant to reign in painless eternity.

But Jesus wouldn't take the rebuke. It defied his sense of his own fate now. He turned on Simon saying "Get behind me, Satan, You're thinking of human things, not God's." But after a while he said to Simon "Simon son of Jonah, now I'll call you Peter" (Peter means *Rock*). And to the other pupils he said "This is Peter and on his shoulders I'll lay my whole plan. The gates of Hell itself won't shake it." Then he went on talking about his fate—pain and death and rising again.

The pupils and even Peter were baffled. They'd waited for places in God's coming reign but now they said nothing.

THEN AFTER six days Jesus took Peter, James and John apart from the others and led them on to the heights of Mount

Hermon. He barely spoke through the arduous climb. Then near the peak and alone in their presence he was changed in form. His clothes turned a very shining white like nothing a human can make on Earth. His face was gleaming and Elijah and Moses were talking with him one at each side.

Peter was cold with fright so he said "Rabbi, it's fine to be here! Let's pitch three tents—one for you, one for Moses and one for Elijah." He didn't know what he was saying. They were terrified.

A cloud came down and covered them and a voice from the cloud said "This is my Son, the one I love. Hear him."

Peter's arms and legs were frozen and he said to himself *I've given too much to this one man and now he shows me this wild sight—me with a home and a hungry family I've left to chase what's either Messiah or the shrewdest demon I've yet known. Should I run for my life or fling myself off this high rock? My family might starve but no one would see my dead shamed face.*

Then suddenly he and the others looked round and saw themselves alone with Jesus.

As they came down the mountain Jesus ordered them to tell no one what they'd seen till the Son of Man should die and rise alive from the dead.

The pupils were baffled but asked him nothing.

As they reached the foot of the mountain they saw a big crowd around the nine other pupils and the usual lawyers were arguing with them.

When the crowd saw Jesus they rushed to greet him. One of them said "Teacher, I've brought you my son who has a dumb spirit. It seizes and flings him. He foams and gnashes his teeth and goes stiff. I told your pupils to help him but they couldn't."

Jesus was angry. He said to the pupils "Disbelievers! How

long must I bear you?" But he told the father to bring the son forward.

They brought the boy forward and, that near Jesus, the spirit shook the boy so hard he fell to the ground and wallowed foaming.

Jesus asked the father how long this had gone on.

The man said "Since childhood. It often throws him into fire or water to kill him. If you can do anything, sir, take pity on us."

Jesus said " 'If you *can*'? Everything *can* be for a believer."

The father cried out "Sir, I believe. Help my unbelief!"

The crowd was pressing closer on them so Jesus hurried and said to the demon "Dumb and deaf spirit, I order you to come out and leave him for good."

Screaming and tearing him hard the demon came out.

The boy looked lifeless.

Many thought he was dead.

But Jesus took his hand, pulled him up and he stood.

When the crowd had scattered the nine pupils asked Jesus why they'd failed to expel the demon.

He said "That kind will only come out for hard prayers."

But when they asked him to teach them a secret powerful prayer he only said what he'd told them before "Our Father in Heaven, your kingdom come. Your will be done on Earth as in Heaven. Give us today the bread we need, forgive us our debts as we forgive our debtors and lead us not to trial but free us from the evil one, amen."

They said "Sir, we prayed as hard as we've ever seen you pray."

He said "Try harder. If your son asks for bread will you give him a stone? If he asks for a fish will you give him a snake? If he asks for an egg will you give him a scorpion?"

So one of them asked if God would ever refuse to hear Jesus.

Jesus said "You don't understand at all, do you?" And though he half smiled he walked far ahead till they were in sight of Nazareth where he'd grown up.

ON THE SABBATH he went to the synagogue there and stood to read. A scroll he'd known since childhood, a text of the prophet Isaiah, was handed to him. Unrolling it Jesus found the place he wanted and read to the crowd,

> *The spirit of the Lord is on me*
> *Because he anointed me*
> *To cheer the poor.*
> *He has sent me announcing release to captives,*
> *Sight to the blind,*
> *Balm to the bruised,*
> *Announcing the welcome year of the Lord.*

Rolling up the scroll and giving it to the keeper Jesus sat and the eyes of all were fixed on him. He began to tell them "Today this scripture is fulfilled in your eyes—"

At first many commended him and wondered at the graceful words from his mouth. They said "Isn't this the builder, Mary's son and the brother of James, Joses, Judas and Simon and aren't his sisters here with us?"

But when he couldn't heal there because some people doubted him Jesus said "Surely you'll tell me 'Do here what you've done in Capernaum.' But I tell you honestly there were many lepers in Israel under Elisha the prophet and not one was healed but Naaman the Syrian. For a prophet is dishonored only in his own town among his own people and in his own house."

All who heard that were filled with rage and rising they led him out of town to the brow of a hill and meant to pitch him over.

But Jesus managed to pass straight through them and go his way.

Behind him the pupils argued among themselves.

WHEN THEY were back in Capernaum, Jesus asked them "What were you arguing on the road?"

They kept silent not wanting him to know that they'd argued who would be first in God's coming reign.

But Jesus knew. He said "If anyone wishes to be first he shall be last of all and the slave of all."

After that he taught them secretly the thing he knew now. He said to all the Twelve that "The Son of Man is betrayed into men's hands. They'll kill him and being killed after three days he'll rise." He told them many times but they couldn't understand. Then though he kept the Twelve with him he sent out seventy other pupils saying that they must go through all Judea now announcing God's coming in every town he meant to visit when he moved south.

The seventy went.

Jesus waited in prayer and hope.

And when they returned they were full of their victory. They said "Sir, even the demons fly from us when we use your name."

Jesus said "Amen then I've seen Satan fall like lightning from Heaven!" For once he exulted.

And those around him watched for the sky to burst with God's full justice and glory. They'd fallen far back of Jesus in understanding his path.

By now it was winter.

So JESUS set his face toward Jerusalem.

The loyal baffled Twelve came behind him—he had that power still.

And on the way a young man ran up and knelt to Jesus saying "Kind teacher, what must I do to win eternal life?"

Jesus said "Why call me kind? No one is kind but God. You know the commandments— *'Do not kill, do not commit adultery, do not steal, do not give false witness, honor your father and mother.'* "

The man said "Teacher, I've done all that."

Gazing at him Jesus loved him and said "One thing's lacking then. Go sell all you own and give it to the poor. You'll have treasure in Heaven. Then follow me."

But the young man was shocked and went away grieving. He had great possessions.

Looking round at the pupils Jesus said "It's easier for a camel to go through the eye of a needle than for a rich man to enter God's reign."

They were puzzled and said among themselves "Then who can be saved?"

Jesus said "With men it's impossible but not with God—everything's possible with God."

Peter started saying "Look, we gave up everything for you—"

But Jesus stopped him. "Amen I tell you there's no one who left home or brothers or sisters or mother or father or children or farms for my sake and the sake of the good news but shall get a hundredfold back in the age to come and eternal life." Again he told them of the Son of Man's fate. Then he turned to walk on.

They were coming to see that by the *Son of Man* he somehow meant himself so they let him precede them by considerable distance. They were stunned and afraid but still they came on.

IT WAS the feast of Dedication and Jerusalem was mobbed with pilgrims to the Temple. Jesus and the pupils stayed east of the city on the Mount of Olives but daily he walked in the porches of the Temple and announced his news to all, Jew or Greek.

Some trusted him at once from the news they'd heard. Others hounded his steps in the hope of trapping him in some blasphemous or seditious claim—everyone in power feared his hold on the poor and outcast.

One group asked him by what right he did his work, who gave him his power?

Jesus said "Answer me one thing and I'll tell you by what right I do my work—John's baptism, was it from God or humankind?"

They reasoned among themselves "If we say 'From God' he'll say 'Then why didn't you obey him?' but if we say 'From men'—they were slow to say that, knowing how the people had honored John. So they said "We don't know."

Jesus said "Then I won't tell you where I get my power."

One of the lawyers knowing he'd answered them well said "Sir, what commandment stands first of all?"

Jesus said "First is *'Hear, Israel, the Lord our God is one Lord and you shall love the Lord your God with all your heart, with all your soul and with all your strength.'* Second is this *'You shall love your neighbor like yourself.'* There's no commandment greater than these."

The lawyer said "True, teacher. There's no other beside God

and to love one's neighbor like oneself is more than all burnt offerings and sacrifices."

Jesus told the man "You're not far from the reign of God."

Then they brought him a woman caught in the very act of adultery. They stood her before him and said "Moses ordered us to stone such a woman. What do you say?"

Jesus stooped and wrote on the ground with his finger as if he hadn't heard them.

So they asked him again.

He stood and said "The one that's sinless among you, let him throw the first stone." Again he stooped and wrote on the ground.

One by one from the oldest to the youngest the men walked off and left Jesus alone with the woman.

Jesus said to her "Woman, where are your accusers? Is no one condemning you?"

She said "No sir."

He said "Neither do I. Go and sin no more."

Later in Solomon's Porch in the Temple he told this story. "A man planted a vineyard, put a fence around it, dug a wine vat and built a watchtower. Then he leased it to tenants and went away. In the summer he sent a slave to the tenants to get some grapes. They beat the slave and sent him away empty handed. The owner sent another slave. They beat his head and insulted him. The owner sent a third. They killed that one and many more—beating some, killing others.

"He had one left, a much-loved son. Finally he sent him to the tenants saying to himself 'They'll honor my son.' But the tenants said to themselves 'Here's the heir. Let's kill him and all the inheritance is ours.' Then they killed the son and flung his body out of the vineyard. What will the owner do? He'll come, kill the tenants and give the vineyard to others."

Some began to see he was speaking of himself and some of

them loved him for it, some meant to arrest him, some to stone him. But they knew he'd told the story on them too. They feared his mob and waited in silence.

So Jesus and the pupils withdrew from Jerusalem and crossed the Jordan beyond the place where John had baptized not two years before.

Many came to Jesus there and trusted in him.

THEN IN BETHANY in the Mount of Olives in sight of the Temple a man named Lazarus fell sick. He was Jesus' friend and the brother of Jesus' friends Mary and Martha. The sisters sent word to Jesus beyond the Jordan and though he loved Lazarus and the sisters he waited two days before saying he'd go to Bethany.

At once the pupils tried to dissuade him. They said "Rabbi, you're in trouble there so near Jerusalem."

Only Thomas was eager. He said "I'm ready to die beside him."

Jesus set out, the others fell in and when they'd passed the Dead Sea and Jericho and climbed the long rise to Bethany, Lazarus had been in the grave four days.

Meeting Jesus on the road Martha even said "Sir, if you'd come sooner he wouldn't have died."

When Mary met him she said the same.

But Jesus walked straight past them to the grave where his friend lay wrapped and cold. When he got there he couldn't conceal his grief. It made him shudder hard and weep.

Many had come from Jerusalem to mourn. They all watched Jesus.

And at last he said "Take the stone off the grave."

Martha said "But sir, he'll stink by now."

They rolled the stone off the dark grave shaft.

Then groaning again and in a loud voice Jesus cried "Lazarus, come out!"

The man who was dead four days came out still wrapped in grave linen.

Jesus kissed him and said "Untie him. Let him live."

All who'd stood by watching were startled. Many trusted in Jesus.

But others went back to Jerusalem and told the chief priests and the ruling council.

Among themselves the council said that if they let Jesus work among them then all the people would follow him and soon the Romans would come and crush them—Jesus, his rabble, the nation around them, the priests and the Temple.

Caiaphas the High Priest finally said "It's better that one man die for the people than that we and all the nation be slaughtered." And from that day the priests and council searched for a way to catch him on safe ground apart from his mob and kill him quickly.

Before they could act Jesus withdrew again, this time to a town named Ephraim north of Jerusalem near the wilderness. He understood that his time was near and more and more he walked out alone and slept apart.

But the Twelve were still with him.

THEN THE TIME for Passover came in early April. Pilgrims moved toward the Temple from all the nation and from foreign lands and the city swelled many times over.

On the first day of Passover week Jesus led the pupils back to the crest of the Mount of Olives. Looking down on the city he called two of them and said "Go to the village opposite and you'll find a tethered colt on which no one's ever sat. Untie it and bring it here. If anyone asks what you're doing say 'The teacher needs it and will send it back at once.'"

Just as he said they found a colt tied to a door outside in the street and they brought it to Jesus, throwing their coats across its back.

Jesus sat on it, rode down the Mount and began the steep climb to the Temple.

Many spread their coats in the road and others spread leafy branches from the fields. The ones in front and those behind cried out *"Hosanna! Blessed is he who comes in the Lord's name!"* Few of them recalled what the prophet Zecharia had said long ago,

> *Rejoice greatly, O daughter Jerusalem!*
> *Look, your king comes to you.*
> *Triumphant and glorious is he,*
> *Humble and riding on an ass,*
> *On a colt the foal of an ass.*

Even the pupils didn't understand though some of the lawyers said to him "Teacher, calm your pupils."

Jesus answered "Amen I tell you if they were silent the stones themselves would cry out."

The priests were only biding their time. Herod was watching. The Romans were watching.

And that night Jesus led his pupils back uphill to Bethany where they dined with Lazarus and his sisters Martha and Mary.

At the end of the meal Mary came forward with a pound of expensive perfumed ointment. She wiped Jesus' feet with it and dried them with her hair. The splendid odor filled the whole house.

Judas was indignant and said "Why wasn't this ointment sold for three hundred dinars and the money given to the poor?"

But Jesus said "You'll have the poor with you always but not me. Let Mary be. She'll keep the remainder to sweeten my corpse." No one but Jesus smiled.

ON THE FOLLOWING morning he entered the Temple courts. He'd brought a stout cord which served as a whip and with it he drove out the merchants, their sacrificial livestock and the moneyhandlers who defiled the place by exchanging money for the Temple tax. As they ran he cried out "Remember it's written *'My house shall be called a house of prayer for all nations.'* But you have made it a bandits' cave."

The priests were watching.

The rest of that day and the next three days as Jesus taught and argued in the Temple his enemies worked to lure him into their trap. They even tried to catch him in sedition. Some lawyers approached him and said "Teacher, we know you're honest and that no one counts heavily with you since you aren't partial to appearances but teach God's way. So tell us is it right to pay tribute to Caesar? Should we pay or not?"

Jesus said "Why tempt me? Show me a coin."

They showed him one.

And he said "Whose picture is this and whose inscription?"

They said "Caesar's."

So he told them "Give Caesar's things back to Caesar. Give God's things to God."

Later to the crowd he denounced the lawyers. "Beware these lawyers. They love to parade in long robes, be bowed to in the market, take the best seats in synagogue and at banquets. Yet they likewise eat up widows' houses under cover of prayer.

They'll get the reward of their pride and their lies." Then turning on the lawyers at hand Jesus said "Great sorrow to you, false teachers. You're like whitewashed tombs that shine in the light but inside are full of dead bones and filth. You're a nest of vipers—who'll save you now? Those who trust me are saved by God's truth. Truth sets them free."

The lawyers said "Look, we're sons of Abraham just like you and have never been slaves. How can you say we're not free?"

Jesus said "Amen I tell you that anyone sinning and sinning again is the slave of sin. I know you claim to be sons of Abraham but you're trying to kill me because I'm bearing the Father's news."

The lawyers said "Our father is Abraham."

Jesus said "Abraham's children do God's will. You're doing the will of your father Satan."

The lawyers laughed. "What's to keep us from saying you're gripped by a demon and mad as a lunatic?"

Jesus said calmly "I know no demons. I honor my Father. You dishonor me. Amen I tell you a final time that anyone hearing and trusting my news will never see death."

The lawyers said "Now we know you're mad. Abraham died, all the prophets died but you're saying 'If anyone trusts me he'll live forever'?"

Jesus nodded and said "Your father Abraham foresaw my day, saw it and delighted."

They laughed again. "You're not even forty and you've seen Abraham?"

Jesus said "Amen amen I tell you before Abraham was I am."

There was rubble handy from the work on the Temple. Many took up stones to throw at Jesus but he managed to leave.

At last though he'd insured his death.

Jesus well knew that. He believed himself. He was on the verge of the fate he'd glimpsed as a boy in school, not to be the glorious warrior chief who'd vanquish the Romans but the sacrificial slave of God whom he'd found foreseen in the prophet Isaiah.

> *He was pierced for our trespasses,*
> *Crushed for our wrongs,*
> *He bore the strokes that left us whole*
> *And by his bruises we are healed.*

ON THE WEDNESDAY Jesus sat with the pupils on the Mount of Olives and looked toward the Temple porches and courts. White marble and gold dazzled in sunlight. Giant hewn stones braced it stronger than any building on Earth. Yet Jesus told the pupils plainly "See those great buildings? There'll be no stone left standing on stone which shall not be toppled."

When the pupils were baffled his feeling deepened and he cried toward the city "O Jerusalem, Jerusalem, killing the prophets and stoning the messengers. How often I'd have gathered your children as a hen gathers her brood to her wings but you wouldn't come. And now the days are strictly numbered till the sun goes dark, the moon fades and all the powers of Heaven quake with the coming trial. For then you'll see the Son of Man coming on clouds with power and glory sending his angels to gather the chosen from pole to pole. He'll separate the souls as a shepherd parts his sheep from the goats—the sheep on his right hand, goats on his left.

"Then the Son will say to those at his right hand 'Come O blessed by my Father. Inherit the kingdom readied for you from the start of the world. For I was hungry and you fed me, thirsty and you gave me drink, I was a stranger and you welcomed me, naked and you clothed me, sick and you visited me, in prison and you came to me.'

"The righteous will say to him 'Lord, when did we see you hungry or thirsty or a stranger or naked and serve you or sick or in prison and visit you?' And the Son will answer them 'Amen I tell you when you did that to the least of my children you did it to me.'

"Those on his left hand will say 'Lord, Lord, haven't we cast out demons in your name and done many wonders? Haven't we kept the law?' But the Son will tell them 'I never knew you. Leave me and enter eternal fire prepared for Satan and his angels for I was hungry and you gave me no food, thirsty and you gave me no drink, a stranger and you never welcomed me, naked and you failed to clothe me, sick and in prison and you never visited me. When you did it to the least of my kin you did it to me.' They'll depart from there into lasting fire but the righteous will enter eternal life."

Thomas asked him when this trial would be.

Jesus said "Amen I tell you that no way shall this generation pass till all these things come down upon you. Heaven and Earth shall pass to dust. My words won't pass. But as to the hour and day none knows, not the angels in Heaven nor even the Son but only the Father. Stay wakeful and watch both day and dark or the Lord may come and find you sleeping."

Peter said "But teacher, who can face the Son? We're common men."

Jesus said "Be perfect like your Father in Heaven."

It made Peter angry the rest of that day.

And late that same night Judas Iscariot who was one of the Twelve went to the priests and offered to betray Jesus' nighttime whereabouts. No one ever knew why he made that choice.

But as the priests heard Judas' offer they were glad and promised him money if he found an occasion to lead them to Jesus when he was alone apart from the mob.

ON THURSDAY which was the first day of unleavened bread when they sacrificed the Passover lamb the pupils said to Jesus "Where do you want us to go and arrange for you to eat the feast?"

He sent two of them saying "Go into the city. You'll be met by a man with a water jug. Follow him. Wherever he enters tell the owner 'The teacher says "Where is my guestroom so I can eat the Passover with my pupils?"' He'll show you a big room upstairs spread and ready. Prepare for us there."

The pupils went out and found the room as he told them.

So as evening fell Jesus came with the Twelve. When they'd taken their places around the table Jesus put off his shirt, wrapped a towel around himself, poured water into a bowl and began to wash the pupils' feet, drying them with the towel at his waist.

He got to Peter but Peter protested "Lord, you'll never wash my feet."

Jesus said to him "If I don't wash you you'll have no part in me."

Peter said "Then not just my feet but my hands and head too."

Jesus washed them all, even Judas who was set on his course now.

As they were eating Jesus said "Amen I tell you one of you will betray me, one eating with me here."

The pupils were distressed and said to one another "Surely not me."

Jesus said "One of you who dips bread into the dish with me— better for that man if he'd not been born."

Then Judas left on his errand. He knew where Jesus would go after this to be apart.

As they finished eating Jesus took a last loaf and blessing it he broke and gave it to them saying "Take. This is my body." Then lifting a cup and giving thanks he gave wine to them.

All drank it.

He said to them "This is my blood of the promise poured out for many. Amen I tell you never in any way will I drink of the fruit of the vine till that day when I drink it new in the reign of God."

After singing a hymn they walked down the side of Zion and up the dry bed of the Kidron brook to a garden at the foot of the Mount of Olives where they'd stayed that week. And Jesus said to them "All of you shall stumble tonight for it's written

I'll strike down the shepherd
And the sheep shall be scattered.

But after I'm raised I'll go ahead of you to Galilee."

They'd still never understood his word *raised*.

But Peter told him "Even if everybody stumbles not I."

Jesus said to Peter "Simon, Simon—look—Satan begged hard to have you to thresh like harvest wheat. I've prayed for you that your faith won't fail."

Peter said "Oh Lord, no way, no way."

Jesus said to him "Amen I tell you—you, today, tonight before the cock crows twice—you'll deny me three times."

But Peter just kept saying "If I must die with you no way would I deny you."

All the others said likewise.

THEY CAME to a plot of land called Gethsemane or "Oil Press." Jesus told the pupils "Sit here while I pray." Taking Peter,

James and John with him he went on farther under the olive trees and began to be deeply appalled and harrowed. He said to the three men "My soul is anguished to death. Stay here and watch."

Going on a little he fell to the ground and prayed that if it were possible the hour might turn away. He said "*Abba*, Father, everything is possible to you. Take this cup from me—still not what I want but you." He came, found the three pupils sleeping and said to Peter "Simon, are you sleeping? Couldn't you watch with me one hour? Watch and pray so you don't come to testing. Oh the spirit is ready but the flesh is weak."

Going back alone Jesus prayed the same words. But the sins of all humankind were laid on his head and at last he felt the weight of the ransom he'd vowed to pay.

This time Peter heard the prayer and saw great drops of sweat like blood on Jesus face. He meant to stand and go toward Jesus but his legs were weak from the long day.

So Jesus came again and found them sleeping since they didn't know how to answer his need.

Once more he pled alone with the Father. Then he came back a third time and said to the three men "Sleep now and rest. It's over. I paid. The hour came. But look, the Son of Man is betrayed into sinners' hands. Get up. Let's go. See, the one who betrays me is nearing."

At once while he was still speaking Judas Iscariot appeared and with him a squad with swords and sticks from the chief priests, lawyers and elders. The traitor had given them a signal—"Whomever I kiss is he. Seize him and take him off securely." Coming up to Jesus then Judas said "Rabbi!" and kissed him lovingly.

The men got their hands on Jesus and bound him.

Peter drew his sword, struck the High Priest's slave and cut off his ear. The man's name was Malchus.

Jesus said to the men "Did you come out armed to arrest a rebel? I was with you every day in the Temple and you didn't seize me."

Deserting him then all the pupils ran.

Only Judas stayed to get his reward.

And one young man who'd followed Jesus was dressed in a linen shirt over his nakedness. The men seized him too but leaving the shirt behind he fled naked.

Then they took Jesus off to the High Priest.

All the chief priests, elders and lawyers gathered.

Peter and John had followed at a distance. They got right into the high Priest's courtyard.

John's family sold salt fish to the Priest so he was known here and could move farther in.

Peter stayed in the courtyard with several slaves and warmed himself by a blaze in the cold night.

NOW THE PRIESTS and the council took testimony from many liars that Jesus had said "I'll tear down this Temple made by hand and after three days I'll build another that's not hand-made." Even so the witnesses were not consistent.

Rising in the center of the chamber the High Priest said to Jesus "Won't you answer to what these men testify?"

But Jesus was silent standing there.

So the High Priest said "Then you are Messiah, the Son of the Blessed?"

Jesus said "I am and you shall see the Son of Man sitting at the right hand of power and coming with clouds of Heaven."

The High Priest tore his robe at that, meaning Jesus had finally sealed his doom.

All the council likewise condemned him to death. Some spat on him, covered his eyes, struck him and said "Now prophesy!"

Even the slaves treated him to blows.

And while Peter was down in the courtyard one of the High Priest's maids saw him warming himself. She said to him "You're with the Nazarene Jesus."

But Peter denied it saying "I don't know him. What are you talking about?" Then he went out to the porch and a cock crowed.

Seeing him the maid said to those standing round "This man is one of them."

Again Peter denied it.

After a little those standing round said to Peter "Surely you're one of them. Anybody can hear you're a Galilean."

Peter began to curse and swear. "I don't even know this man you mention." Then a second time the cock crowed and Peter remembered Jesus saying "Before the cock crows twice you'll deny me three times" and dwelling on that he wept bitterly.

In the morning the priests, the lawyers, the elders and all the council handed Jesus over to Pilate at Roman headquarters in the former palace of Herod the Great by the western gate. For fear of defiling themselves that day and being unfit to eat the Passover they stayed outside while the soldiers led Jesus.

Pilate asked him "You're the king of the Jews?"

Jesus said "You say."

Pilate asked him "Then what have you done? Are you some zealot?"

Jesus said "My domain is not here and now. If it were my friends would fight for me."

Pilate said "So you are a king?"

Jesus said again "You know the truth."

Pilate said "What's the truth?"

Jesus said no more.

Then Pilate went out to the waiting accusers and said "You

have your custom that I free one prisoner at every feast. Do you want me to free the King of the Jews?"

They all cried "Barabbas! No, give us Barabbas." Barabbas was a bandit.

Pilate said "Then what must I do with Jesus?"

They cried "Crucify him!"

So Pilate had the soldiers take Jesus and whip him. Then they dressed him in a royal purple robe, plaited a crown of thorns for his head, saluted him as King of the Jews, mocked and spat on him and returned him to Pilate.

Pilate led Jesus back outside. To the waiting accusers he said "Here's the man."

They only cried again "Crucify him!"

Pilate handed Jesus to a squad of soldiers who stripped him of his robe, laid the arm piece of his cross on his shoulders and led him north through the city to die. When Jesus stumbled under the weight they forced one Simon from Cyrene to bear it.

So they went north through the Gennath gate and came to the hill Golgotha, "Skull Place," in a limestone quarry long since worked out. They gave Jesus wine that was drugged with myrrh, a small mercy. Then they stripped him naked, nailed his arms and feet to the cross and hoisted the cross with him upright. At his head they nailed the charge against him written in Latin, Hebrew and Greek. It said "Jesus of Nazareth King of the Jews." Below him as was their privilege the soldiers divided his clothes. His coat was woven in a single piece so rather than tear it they cast lots for it. Then at Jesus' right and left they crucified two thieves. It was about noon.

The passersby insulted Jesus by wagging their heads and saying "So!—the man who'd destroy the Temple and build it in three days. Save yourself. Step down from the cross."

The chief priests also watched and mocked him.

Even the thieves beside him cursed him.

None of his friends were near at hand. Only the women who'd followed from Galilee stood at a distance watching in grief. Among them were Mary from Magdala, Mary the mother of the younger James and Joses, and Salome. They tried to console his mother who was with them.

A great darkness settled on the place and at three in the afternoon Jesus shouted in a loud voice " *'Eloi, Eloi, lama sabachthani?'* It means "My God, my God why did you desert me?"

Some of the bystanders thought he was calling Elijah. One of them ran, filled a sponge with vinegar, put it on a stick and held it up to his mouth to drink saying "Let's see now if Elijah saves him."

No one saved him.

Toward three o'clock the sky went dark.

Jesus cried out loud again and breathed his last.

Since the priests had a rule against leaving dead men on their crosses after sundown, above all on the Sabbath, the soldiers came in late afternoon to break the legs of Jesus and the thieves. It would speed their deaths since they couldn't press up on their feet to breathe. When the soldiers reached Jesus he seemed to be dead. For certainty one soldier pierced his side with a spear.

Blood and water poured out. He was long since dead.

Sundown Friday was coming fast—the preparation for the Sabbath—so Joseph from Arimathea, an important member of the council who likewise expected God's coming reign, went boldly to Pilate and asked for Jesus' body.

Pilate wondered if he was already dead and called the captain of the hanging party.

The captain confirmed it.

So Pilate presented the corpse to Joseph.

Quickly buying new linen and hauling Jesus down from the cross Joseph hurried to wrap him in the linen with spices. Near the cross was a garden where Joseph's own family tomb was waiting—it had never been used. They laid Jesus there and rolled a heavy stone to the entrance.

The two younger Marys watched where he was put. They'd come back after the Sabbath to finish washing the body. With all the rules against work on the Sabbath that could be no sooner than dark on Saturday or Sunday dawn.

AT DAYLIGHT Sunday morning the two Marys and Salome returned to the tomb with cloths and spices to wash and anoint Jesus' body. All the way they asked themselves "Who'll roll back the stone?"—the stone was huge. But when they reached the actual tomb the stone was rolled back. The entrance was open. Two of the women balked in fear.

Mary from Magdala walked forward though, telling herself at every step *The world is frozen now in death. At last the demons have fouled his body. Even my hand that would wash his corpse is helpless in chill air before me. All my life has passed by useless.* When she took the last step she saw a young man on the right of the tomb where the corpse had lain when she last saw it.

The man wore a white coat and when he saw Mary near he said "Don't be afraid. Are you hunting Jesus the dead Nazarene? He was raised. He's gone. Go tell all his pupils and Peter that he's going ahead to Galilee. You'll see him there as he told you before."

Going out again the women fled. They were shuddering and wild with shock and for a cold hour they told no one nothing.

When the women finally broke their story the pupils doubted and feared a trap.

43

But Peter and John ran toward the tomb.

John got there first, stopped at the entrance and bent to look in. He saw the linen lying empty.

Peter went straight in, saw the linen and also the face cloth apart from the linen and folded neatly.

John went in then, examined the linen and believed. Then he and Peter returned to where the pupils had hid for fear of their enemies.

But Mary from Magdala had followed them back to the tomb and now she stood alone weeping at the entrance.

A man behind her said "Woman, why weep?"

Mary turned but didn't know him as Jesus. She thought he was a gardener. She said "Sir, if you've taken him show me where."

The man said "Mary—"

Then she knew. She cried out "Rabbi!" and knelt to clasp his knees.

Jesus said "Stop holding me" and raised her upright. Then he told her plainly what to tell the pupils—he was risen indeed.

WITH THAT NEWS the pupils were even more amazed. They stayed in hiding afraid and uncertain. But that night when they'd finished eating Jesus suddenly stood in their midst— the door had been locked. They were terrified and thought he was a ghost.

He said "No fear. I am—look." He showed them the holes in his wrists and feet and the wound in his side. Then he asked for something to eat. They brought him part of a broiled fish and a comb of honey and he ate in plain view. Then he told them again he was bound for Galilee.

After that Jesus showed himself unmistakably to James his brother and to Judas the traitor who then went out to the field he'd bought with his blood money and hanged himself. Jesus likewise appeared unquestionably to upward of five hundred people who'd known him. It was later in Galilee that he left the remaining pupils.

PETER AND ANDREW, James and John sons of Zebedee, Thomas, Nathanael and two more pupils returned to Capernaum to wait for his coming as the Son in glory. One night Simon said "I'm going fishing."

The others said "We're coming with you."

They went out, got into the boat and all that night caught nothing.

But when it was dawn Jesus stood on the shore, not that the pupils knew it was Jesus.

Jesus called to them "Boys, nothing to eat?"

They called back "No."

He said "Cast to starboard. You'll find some."

They cast the net and then could barely drag it there were so many fish.

John said to Peter "It's the Lord."

Peter hearing that tucked his coat up—under it he was naked—and threw himself into the lake.

But even in sight of Jesus again the other pupils came on in the boat hauling the lucky net of fish. They were only a hundred yards from shore. When they landed they saw a charcoal fire laid, a fish lying on it and bread.

Jesus said to them "Bring some of your fish."

Peter got up—he'd been panting in the shallows—and helped beach the net. They'd caught a hundred fifty-three fish but the net wasn't torn.

Jesus said "Come eat."

None of the pupils dared ask him "Who are you?" knowing it was Jesus raised from the dead.

When they'd eaten in silence Jesus pointed to all the men and said to Peter "Simon son of Jonah do you love me more than these?"

He said "Yes Lord, I love you."

Jesus said "Feed my lambs." Then a second time he said "Simon son of Jonah do you love me?"

Peter said "Yes Lord, you know I love you."

Jesus said "Tend my young sheep." A third time he said "Simon son of Jonah do you love me?"

Not understanding that Jesus was letting him cancel each of his three denials Peter was grieved that he'd asked him a third time. He said "Lord, you know everything. You know I love you."

Jesus said again "Tend my young sheep."

Peter nodded yes and took more bread.

The other pupils watched in silence.

Then Jesus rose and walked away to the east in the new light of that last day.

It had been two years since they first met him and they'd never see him again on Earth. It would only be slowly that they came to see how in the time they shared his life, his hard ordeal and calm return had ended things as they'd been from the start. He'd reconciled an angry God to them and their kind, all human creatures. And whatever they lacked that final dawn they gave the rest of their lives to his other task, the task he failed—to make all people know that God is at hand—and they never lost hope to see him come again on clouds in the Father's power to claim them at last. One of their cries in their own language was *Maranatha*—"Lord, come now!" They thought he had promised that.

In other lives their cry has lasted near two thousand years.

This book is set in Linotype Granjon
with Goudy's Garamont Light used for display.
Typesetting and printing by Heritage Printers, Inc.
Design by Jonathan Greene. Published in an
edition of seven hundred copies, of which
five hundred are for sale. The first
hundred, specially bound,
are signed by the
author.

Copy: 418

418